EMMANUEL JOSEPH

The Minds Behind the Empires, Personal Stories of Tech and Real Estate Titans

Copyright © 2025 by Emmanuel Joseph

All rights reserved. No part of this publication may be reproduced, stored or transmitted in any form or by any means, electronic, mechanical, photocopying, recording, scanning, or otherwise without written permission from the publisher. It is illegal to copy this book, post it to a website, or distribute it by any other means without permission.

First edition

This book was professionally typeset on Reedsy.
Find out more at reedsy.com

Contents

1	Chapter 1: Beginnings of Brilliance	1
2	Chapter 2: A Vision Takes Shape	3
3	Chapter 3: The First Triumphs	5
4	Chapter 4: Building an Empire	7
5	Chapter 5: Innovating the Future	9
6	Chapter 6: Leadership and Legacy	11
7	Chapter 7: Facing Adversity	13
8	Chapter 8: Personal Sacrifices	15
9	Chapter 9: The Role of Mentorship	17
10	Chapter 10: Social Impact and Responsibility	19
11	Chapter 11: Reflections on Success	21
12	Chapter 12: Inspiring the Next Generation	23

1

Chapter 1: Beginnings of Brilliance

In every empire, there's a spark of ingenuity. This chapter delves into the early lives of our tech and real estate titans, tracing their humble beginnings. Many faced overwhelming odds, but their drive and determination set them on the path to greatness. Their childhood dreams, education, and first steps into their respective industries are detailed, showing that every success story starts with a single step.

For many of these titans, their early years were marked by modesty and struggle. Growing up in small towns or bustling cities, they encountered challenges that would shape their resolve. Some were inspired by their parents' entrepreneurial spirit, while others found their passion through early exposure to technology or real estate. These experiences, though diverse, laid the foundation for their future endeavors.

As they pursued their education, these future leaders demonstrated exceptional talent and curiosity. Whether it was excelling in science and mathematics or developing a keen eye for architecture and design, their academic journeys were filled with moments of discovery. Teachers and mentors played pivotal roles in nurturing their potential, encouraging them to explore their interests and push the boundaries of what they could achieve.

The transition from education to professional life was not always smooth. Many of our titans faced significant setbacks and rejections in their early careers. However, these obstacles only fueled their determination to succeed.

Through perseverance and resilience, they seized opportunities to prove themselves, often taking on challenging projects or starting their ventures from scratch. These formative experiences taught them invaluable lessons about grit and innovation.

Ultimately, it was their unwavering belief in their vision that propelled them forward. Each titan had a unique spark that drove them to pursue their dreams relentlessly. Their early triumphs and the lessons they learned along the way became the building blocks of their empires. As we delve deeper into their stories, we will see how these humble beginnings were just the starting point for their extraordinary journeys.

2

Chapter 2: A Vision Takes Shape

Vision is the cornerstone of every empire. In this chapter, we explore the formative moments when our titans' ideas began to crystallize. Whether it's the groundbreaking technology that redefined communication or the revolutionary real estate development that reshaped a skyline, these moments are where the spark of genius began to shine.

For our tech innovators, their visions often emerged from a desire to solve pressing problems or enhance everyday experiences. Inspired by the rapid advancements in computing and connectivity, they saw opportunities to create something transformative. It might have been during a late-night coding session, a chance encounter with a mentor, or a flash of insight while observing a common inconvenience. These epiphanies set them on a path to explore uncharted territories.

On the real estate front, the visionaries were driven by a passion for creating spaces that would stand the test of time and elevate the human experience. They imagined buildings that weren't just structures, but landmarks that defined cityscapes and communities. Their ideas often took shape through countless sketches, discussions with architects, and walks through bustling urban centers. These early conceptualizations laid the groundwork for their grand projects.

The journey from vision to reality was filled with challenges. Many faced skepticism from peers, financial constraints, and technical hurdles. Yet, their unwavering belief in their ideas pushed them forward. They sought out collaborators who shared their enthusiasm and could bring their visions to life. Through perseverance, they gradually turned abstract concepts into tangible prototypes and blueprints.

Key to this process was the ability to see potential where others saw obstacles. Our titans had a unique knack for identifying opportunities and taking calculated risks. They were not afraid to pivot when necessary, adapting their visions to better align with emerging trends and technologies. This flexibility and foresight were crucial in navigating the uncertain waters of innovation.

In essence, the crystallization of their visions was a blend of inspiration, hard work, and a deep understanding of their fields. As they moved from ideas to implementation, the foundation of their empires began to take shape. Their stories remind us that vision is not just about seeing the future—it's about creating it, one step at a time.

3

Chapter 3: The First Triumphs

No empire is built overnight. This chapter focuses on the early successes that gave our titans the momentum they needed. Through hard work, innovation, and sometimes a bit of luck, these pioneers made their first mark on the world. The joy of these initial victories and the lessons learned from their first setbacks are shared, painting a picture of resilience and relentless pursuit.

For our tech pioneers, their first triumphs often came in the form of breakthrough products or software that captured the public's imagination. These early successes were not just about financial gain—they validated the potential of their ideas and provided the encouragement needed to pursue even greater ambitions. The thrill of seeing their creations used and appreciated by people worldwide was a profound motivator.

In the real estate domain, the first triumphs often involved completing significant projects that transformed neighborhoods and cities. These initial developments showcased their ability to turn visions into reality, creating spaces that were both functional and aesthetically pleasing. The pride of watching their projects come to life, from blueprints to bustling communities, fueled their desire to take on more ambitious undertakings.

However, these early successes were not without their challenges. Many faced setbacks and failures along the way, but these obstacles only strengthened their resolve. They learned to adapt, innovate, and overcome, using each experience as a stepping stone toward future successes. Their ability to navigate the complexities of their industries set them apart as true leaders.

The stories of these first triumphs also highlight the importance of collaboration. Our titans understood that building an empire required the support and expertise of others. They formed partnerships, built strong teams, and fostered a culture of innovation and excellence. These relationships were crucial in turning their early achievements into lasting success.

Ultimately, the first triumphs were more than just milestones—they were the foundation upon which their empires were built. These early victories demonstrated the power of vision, determination, and collaboration, setting the stage for the remarkable journeys that followed.

4

Chapter 4: Building an Empire

Constructing a lasting empire requires more than just vision—it needs strategy. This chapter delves into the strategic moves, from mergers and acquisitions to groundbreaking projects, that cemented these leaders' places in history. Their stories reveal the intricate planning and bold decisions that turned their visions into reality.

For our tech titans, strategic decisions often involved scaling their operations and expanding their product lines. They identified key opportunities for growth, whether through entering new markets or developing complementary technologies. These moves required careful planning and a deep understanding of their industry landscapes. Their ability to anticipate trends and adapt to changing conditions was crucial in maintaining their competitive edge.

In the real estate sector, strategy played a vital role in selecting and developing prime locations. Our titans had a keen eye for spotting potential in underdeveloped areas and transforming them into thriving communities. They navigated complex regulatory environments, secured financing, and managed large-scale construction projects. Their strategic acumen enabled them to create iconic developments that redefined urban living.

The process of building an empire also involved taking calculated risks. Our titans were not afraid to invest in innovative ideas or make bold moves that others might have considered too risky. Their willingness to embrace uncertainty and push boundaries set them apart from their peers. These strategic risks often led to breakthrough successes that solidified their positions as industry leaders.

Collaboration and partnerships were essential components of their strategies. Our titans understood the value of forming alliances with other industry leaders, investors, and innovators. These partnerships provided access to resources, expertise, and new opportunities. By working together, they were able to achieve more than they could have alone.

Ultimately, building an empire is a testament to the power of strategic thinking and bold decision-making. Our titans' ability to plan, adapt, and execute their strategies with precision enabled them to turn their visions into reality. Their stories highlight the importance of foresight, collaboration, and resilience in achieving lasting success.

5

Chapter 5: Innovating the Future

Innovation is the lifeblood of tech and real estate empires. In this chapter, we explore how our titans continued to push the boundaries of what's possible. From pioneering new technologies to reimagining urban landscapes, their relentless drive for innovation kept their empires at the forefront of their industries.

For our tech innovators, the pursuit of innovation was a constant journey. They invested heavily in research and development, fostering a culture of creativity and experimentation within their companies. This commitment to innovation led to the creation of groundbreaking products and services that transformed the way people live and work. From advancements in artificial intelligence to cutting-edge software solutions, their contributions have left an indelible mark on the tech landscape.

In the realm of real estate, innovation took the form of visionary architecture and sustainable development practices. Our titans were pioneers in creating green buildings, smart cities, and mixed-use developments that catered to the evolving needs of urban populations. Their projects not only pushed the boundaries of design but also prioritized environmental sustainability and community well-being. These innovations set new standards for the industry and inspired others to follow suit.

The journey of innovation was not without its challenges. Our titans often faced resistance to change and skepticism from traditionalists. However, their unwavering belief in the power of innovation propelled them forward. They embraced new technologies, explored unconventional ideas, and took risks that others might have avoided. Their willingness to experiment and learn from failures was a key factor in their success.

Collaboration and interdisciplinary thinking were also crucial to their innovative endeavors. Our titans recognized the value of bringing together diverse perspectives and expertise. They formed partnerships with researchers, designers, and other innovators to tackle complex challenges and develop holistic solutions. This collaborative approach enabled them to stay ahead of the curve and drive continuous improvement.

Ultimately, innovation is about creating a better future. Our titans' relentless pursuit of new ideas and their commitment to pushing the boundaries of what is possible have had a profound impact on their industries and the world at large. Their stories remind us that true innovation requires courage, curiosity, and a willingness to challenge the status quo.

6

Chapter 6: Leadership and Legacy

Great leaders inspire greatness in others. This chapter examines the leadership styles and philosophies that set these titans apart. Their approaches to mentorship, company culture, and social responsibility offer insights into how they nurtured talent and built lasting legacies beyond their empires.

For our tech leaders, effective leadership involved fostering a culture of innovation and inclusivity. They understood the importance of empowering their teams, encouraging creativity, and providing the resources needed to pursue bold ideas. Their leadership styles were characterized by open communication, a willingness to listen, and a commitment to continuous learning. By creating an environment where people could thrive, they attracted top talent and drove their companies to new heights.

In the real estate sector, leadership was about envisioning and executing large-scale projects that made a lasting impact on communities. Our titans prioritized collaboration, transparency, and ethical practices in their dealings with stakeholders. They recognized the importance of building trust and maintaining strong relationships with partners, clients, and residents. Their leadership extended beyond their companies, as they championed initiatives that promoted social and environmental responsibility.

Mentorship played a significant role in shaping their legacies. Our titans were committed to guiding the next generation of leaders, sharing their knowledge, and providing opportunities for growth. They understood that investing in people was the key to sustaining their empires and creating a lasting impact. Through formal mentorship programs and informal guidance, they helped nurture the talents of future innovators and changemakers.

Corporate social responsibility was also a core component of their leadership philosophies. Our titans believed in giving back to the communities that supported their success. They launched initiatives that addressed social issues, supported education, and promoted environmental sustainability. Their philanthropic efforts reflected their commitment to making a positive difference in the world and leaving a legacy that extended beyond their business achievements.

Ultimately, leadership is about more than just achieving success—it's about inspiring others, making a positive impact, and leaving a lasting legacy. Our titans' leadership styles and philosophies have set them apart as true visionaries. Their stories highlight the importance of empathy, integrity, and a commitment to nurturing talent and promoting social good.

7

Chapter 7: Facing Adversity

E very empire faces challenges, and our titans are no different. This chapter recounts the toughest trials they've encountered—from economic downturns to personal losses—and how they overcame them. Their stories of resilience, adaptability, and perseverance are a testament to the strength required to maintain an empire.

Economic downturns and market fluctuations posed significant challenges for our tech and real estate leaders. During periods of financial instability, they had to make difficult decisions to keep their companies afloat. Whether it was cutting costs, pivoting business strategies, or seeking new revenue streams, their ability to adapt and remain focused on their long-term vision was crucial. These experiences taught them the importance of resilience and the need to be proactive in navigating uncertain times.

Personal losses and health challenges also tested their resolve. Many of our titans faced moments of deep personal struggle, whether due to illness, the loss of loved ones, or other life-altering events. Despite these hardships, they found ways to persevere and continue leading their empires. Their stories of overcoming personal adversity serve as powerful reminders of the human spirit's strength and the importance of maintaining a balance between personal well-being and professional responsibilities.

Regulatory and legal obstacles were another common challenge. Our titans often had to navigate complex legal landscapes, secure necessary permits, and comply with evolving regulations. These hurdles required a thorough understanding of the legal environment and the ability to work collaboratively with regulators and policymakers. Their ability to navigate these challenges demonstrated their tenacity and strategic thinking.

Innovation also came with its own set of challenges. Pushing the boundaries of what was possible often meant facing skepticism and resistance from traditionalists. Our titans had to advocate for their ideas, secure funding, and demonstrate the value of their innovations. This required a combination of persuasive communication, data-driven decision-making, and a steadfast belief Innovation also came with its own set of challenges. Pushing the boundaries of what was possible often meant facing skepticism and resistance from traditionalists. Our titans had to advocate for their ideas, secure funding, and demonstrate the value of their innovations. This required a combination of persuasive communication, data-driven decision-making, and a steadfast belief in their vision. Their ability to overcome these obstacles and remain focused on their goals was a testament to their resilience and determination.

Adversity also brought opportunities for growth and transformation. Many of our titans used difficult times as a catalyst for change, reevaluating their strategies and finding new ways to innovate. They embraced a mindset of continuous improvement, learning from their experiences and adapting to new realities. This ability to turn challenges into opportunities for growth was a defining characteristic of their leadership.

Ultimately, facing adversity is an inherent part of building and maintaining an empire. Our titans' stories of resilience, adaptability, and perseverance demonstrate the strength required to navigate the complexities of their industries. Their experiences serve as powerful reminders that challenges are not obstacles to success but opportunities for growth and transformation.

8

Chapter 8: Personal Sacrifices

Behind every success, there are personal sacrifices. This chapter reveals the often unseen struggles our titans faced in their personal lives. Balancing family, health, and personal happiness with the demands of their empires required tough decisions and deep introspection.

For many of our tech leaders, the relentless pursuit of their vision often meant long hours and intense workloads. The demands of building and scaling a tech empire left little time for personal pursuits and relationships. Some faced the strain of maintaining work-life balance, and their stories highlight the personal sacrifices they made to achieve their goals. These sacrifices were not always easy, but they were driven by a deep passion for their work and a commitment to making a lasting impact.

In the real estate sector, the pressures of managing large-scale projects and navigating complex regulatory environments took a toll on personal well-being. Our titans often had to travel extensively, spending time away from their families and loved ones. The stress of overseeing multiple projects and ensuring their successful completion added to the challenges they faced. Despite these sacrifices, their dedication to their vision and their desire to create lasting legacies kept them motivated.

Health challenges were another aspect of their personal sacrifices. The physical and mental demands of their roles often took a toll on their well-being. Many of our titans experienced burnout, stress-related health issues, and the need to prioritize self-care. Their stories underscore the importance of maintaining a balance between professional success and personal health, and the steps they took to manage their well-being.

Relationships also played a significant role in their journeys. Our titans' personal lives were shaped by the support and understanding of their families, partners, and friends. The sacrifices they made often involved missing important family events or compromising on personal time. However, the support and encouragement they received from their loved ones were crucial in helping them navigate these challenges.

Ultimately, personal sacrifices are an integral part of the journey to success. Our titans' stories highlight the complexities of balancing personal and professional lives and the resilience required to overcome these challenges. Their experiences remind us that true success is not just about achieving professional milestones but also about finding harmony between work and personal fulfillment.

9

Chapter 9: The Role of Mentorship

No one builds an empire alone. Here, we explore the mentors who guided our titans and the importance of mentorship in their journeys. These relationships provided invaluable support, wisdom, and encouragement, shaping the leaders they became.

For our tech innovators, mentorship played a pivotal role in their development. From early influences to seasoned industry veterans, mentors provided guidance, shared their experiences, and offered insights that helped shape their career paths. These relationships were built on trust, mutual respect, and a shared passion for innovation. Mentors not only provided technical expertise but also helped our titans navigate the challenges of leadership and entrepreneurship.

In the real estate sector, mentorship was equally important. Our titans benefited from the wisdom and experience of established developers, architects, and industry leaders. These mentors provided valuable advice on project management, negotiation, and strategic decision-making. Their guidance helped our titans build their networks, refine their visions, and navigate the complexities of the real estate industry.

Mentorship was not just about receiving guidance—it was also about giving back. Our titans understood the importance of paying it forward and became mentors themselves. They invested time and resources in nurturing the next generation of leaders, providing opportunities for growth and development.

By sharing their knowledge and experiences, they helped shape the future of their industries and inspired others to pursue their dreams.

The impact of mentorship extended beyond professional development. Mentors provided emotional support, encouragement, and a sense of community. They helped our titans stay grounded, motivated, and focused on their goals. These relationships were a source of inspiration and strength, offering a sense of camaraderie and shared purpose.

Ultimately, mentorship is a vital component of success. Our titans' stories highlight the importance of seeking guidance, building meaningful relationships, and giving back to others. Their experiences remind us that mentorship is a powerful force for growth, learning, and achieving greatness.

10

Chapter 10: Social Impact and Responsibility

Empires are not just about wealth and power—they're about influence. This chapter discusses the social contributions and philanthropic efforts of our titans. Their commitment to giving back to their communities and making a positive impact on society highlights the broader responsibilities of leadership.

For our tech leaders, social impact was a core value. They leveraged their success and resources to address pressing social issues, from education and healthcare to environmental sustainability. Their philanthropic efforts included funding scholarships, supporting research initiatives, and launching programs to bridge the digital divide. Their commitment to making a positive difference extended beyond their businesses and into the lives of countless individuals.

In the real estate sector, our titans focused on creating sustainable and inclusive communities. They prioritized affordable housing, green building practices, and community development initiatives. Their projects aimed to improve the quality of life for residents, promote economic growth, and foster a sense of community. Their dedication to social responsibility was reflected in their efforts to create spaces that were not only functional but also enriched the lives of those who lived and worked in them.

Corporate social responsibility was a key aspect of their leadership philosophies. Our titans recognized the importance of ethical practices, transparency, and accountability. They championed initiatives that promoted diversity, equity, and inclusion within their organizations and the broader community. Their efforts to create inclusive workplaces and support underrepresented groups set new standards for corporate responsibility.

Collaboration with non-profit organizations, governments, and other stakeholders was essential to their social impact efforts. Our titans formed partnerships to address complex social challenges and drive meaningful change. These collaborations enabled them to leverage their expertise, resources, and networks to create a broader and more lasting impact.

Ultimately, social impact and responsibility are integral to the legacy of our titans. Their stories highlight the importance of using wealth and influence for the greater good. Their commitment to giving back, promoting sustainability, and creating inclusive communities serves as an inspiration for future leaders.

11

Chapter 11: Reflections on Success

What does success truly mean? In this chapter, our titans reflect on their journeys, sharing their definitions of success and the values that guided them. Their insights offer a deeper understanding of what it takes to build and sustain an empire.

For many of our tech leaders, success was not just about financial achievements but about making a meaningful impact. They valued innovation, creativity, and the ability to solve real-world problems. Their reflections emphasized the importance of staying true to their vision, taking risks, and embracing a mindset of continuous learning. Success, for them, was about creating something that made a difference in the world and left a lasting legacy.

In the real estate sector, success was defined by the ability to transform spaces and improve communities. Our titans took pride in their projects' impact on the urban landscape and the lives of residents. They valued sustainability, inclusivity, and the creation of vibrant, livable spaces. Their reflections highlighted the importance of balancing aesthetic and functional considerations with social and environmental responsibility.

Personal fulfillment was also a significant aspect of their definitions of success. Our titans reflected on the importance of achieving a balance between professional accomplishments and personal well-being. They valued the support of their families, the joy of meaningful relationships, and the satisfaction of personal growth. Their stories emphasized that true success is multifaceted and includes both personal and professional fulfillment.

Legacy was another key theme in their reflections. Our titans were deeply committed to leaving a positive and lasting impact on their industries and communities. They valued mentorship, philanthropy, and the ability to inspire future generations. Their reflections underscored the importance of thinking beyond immediate gains and considering the long-term impact of their actions.

Ultimately, success is a deeply personal and evolving concept. Our titans' reflections remind us that there is no single definition of success and that it is shaped by individual values, experiences, and aspirations. Their stories offer valuable insights into the diverse and multifaceted nature of success.

12

Chapter 12: Inspiring the Next Generation

As we conclude our journey, this chapter looks to the future. Our titans share their advice for aspiring leaders and the next generation of innovators. Their stories serve as a source of inspiration, encouraging others to dream big, take risks, and make their mark on the world.

For our tech leaders, the message was clear: embrace curiosity, take risks, and never stop learning. They emphasized the importance of staying adaptable, being open to new ideas, and continuously seeking opportunities for growth. Their advice highlighted the value of perseverance, resilience, and the willingness to challenge the status quo. They encouraged aspiring leaders to be bold, innovative, and unafraid to pursue their passions.

In the real estate sector, the focus was on the importance of vision, collaboration, and sustainability. Our titans advised aspiring leaders to think big, work together, and prioritize creating lasting, positive impacts on communities. They emphasized the value of strategic planning, ethical practices, and continuous innovation. Their stories highlighted the importance of being adaptable, learning from failures, and maintaining a commitment to excellence.

Both tech and real estate leaders stressed the importance of mentorship and lifelong learning. They encouraged aspiring innovators to seek out mentors, build strong networks, and remain open to new experiences and knowledge. They shared the importance of staying curious, asking questions, and never being afraid to challenge conventional wisdom. Their advice reflected the belief that true leadership is about empowering others and fostering a culture of growth and development.

Our titans also spoke about the importance of resilience and perseverance. They reminded aspiring leaders that the journey to success is filled with challenges and setbacks, but it is through overcoming these obstacles that true growth occurs. They encouraged the next generation to stay focused on their goals, remain adaptable, and never give up on their dreams. Their stories of resilience and determination serve as powerful examples of what can be achieved with persistence and hard work.

The final piece of advice from our titans was to stay true to one's values and vision. They emphasized the importance of maintaining integrity, being authentic, and leading with purpose. They reminded aspiring leaders that true success is not just about financial achievements but about making a positive impact on the world and leaving a lasting legacy. Their stories inspire us to dream big, take risks, and strive for greatness.

As we conclude this journey through the lives of tech and real estate titans, we are reminded of the power of vision, innovation, and resilience. Their stories serve as a source of inspiration for aspiring leaders and innovators, encouraging them to pursue their passions, overcome challenges, and make their mark on the world. The minds behind these empires have left an indelible legacy, and their journeys continue to inspire the next generation of trailblazers.

The Minds Behind the Empires: Personal Stories of Tech and Real Estate Titans

This captivating book takes you on an intimate journey into the lives of some of the most influential figures in the worlds of technology and real estate. Through personal stories and behind-the-scenes insights, you'll discover the sparks of ingenuity that set these titans on their paths to greatness. From humble beginnings and the challenges they faced to their groundbreaking

CHAPTER 12: INSPIRING THE NEXT GENERATION

innovations and lasting legacies, this book delves into the minds of those who reshaped our world.

Each chapter offers a unique glimpse into their formative experiences, visionary ideas, and strategic decisions that turned dreams into reality. You'll read about their first triumphs, the struggles they overcame, and the personal sacrifices they made along the way. The role of mentorship, the impact of their leadership, and their commitment to social responsibility are also explored, providing a holistic view of what it takes to build and sustain an empire.

This book is not just a collection of success stories—it's a source of inspiration for anyone aspiring to make their mark on the world. Whether you're an entrepreneur, a student, or simply someone who loves a good story, "The Minds Behind the Empires" offers valuable lessons and a renewed appreciation for the power of vision, innovation, and resilience.

www.ingramcontent.com/pod-product-compliance
Lightning Source LLC
LaVergne TN
LVHW010445070526
838199LV00066B/6206